The Journey Principles™

YOUR JOURNEY, GOD'S PRINCIPLES

C●nnect the D●ts

A SMALL GROUP STUDY GUIDE

by
Nathan Snapp & Stephen Scoggins
©2015

JOURNEY PRINCIPLES INSTITUTE, INC. PUBLISHING

Journey Principles Institute, Inc. Publishing
423 E. 2nd Street
Clayton, NC 27520
www.stephenscoggins.com
www.journeyprinciples.com

Ordering information: Quantity sales. Special discounts are available on quantity purchases by corporations, associations, and others. For details, contact the publisher at the address above. Orders on-line with various trade bookstores and wholesalers such as Amazon: www.amazon.com.

Printed in the United States of America

Connect the Dots: A Small Group Study Guide / Nathan Snapp & Stephen Scoggins.
ISBN10: 0-9862783-6-X
ISBN13: 978-0-9862783-6-5
Non-fiction: Motivational, Self-Help and Spiritual. First Edition

Cover and interior design by Jeff Lawson, Cowan Graphic Design, Inc.

The Journey Principles™

YOUR JOURNEY, GOD'S PRINCIPLES

TABLE OF CONTENTS

The Journey Principles
Connect The Dots

Introduction by Nathan Snapp

I have learned that life is simply a series of choices. If you took those lifepoints and plotted them out on a sheet of paper and then drew a line connecting them, much like the connect-the-dots drawings you did when you were a kid, you would have an outline of you. Everything inside of the lines, every choice, every action or reaction, is what makes you who you are.

Close your eyes for a moment and imagine you are looking at a connect-the-dots exercise that was just completed by an eight-year-old. If I asked you what it is that you were looking at you would base your description on the plot points and the outline that had been created. Hopefully, if the child followed the numbers correctly, you would have a very good idea of what that picture was supposed to be. But what if I asked you what the child believed the picture was going to be before they started drawing? What if I asked you to explain why they chose that particular color crayon? Why is their banana orange, why is their snowman green, and if the picture turned out to be a horse how come they colored in the background to look like it was beneath the sea rather than a meadow? You see, when others look at your lifepoints they don't get to see your imagination. They don't get to see your train of thought. They don't have a detailed description of your belief system. And, unless they have been in your life since point one, they don't have the slightest idea of the unique journey and circumstances that have shaped and molded you and brought you into this specific moment in time. However, the unfortunate thing that everyone eventually realizes is that, even though no one else in the world has access to all of your information, it will not stop them from taking the information that they do have, attempting to connect-the-dots, and slapping a label

5

on the picture that they believe they see. Unfair? To some degree yes, but just like you, every other person in the world is taking the limited information they have been given and searching for a way to apply it to their own personal experience so that they can reason and rationalize, attempting to cling to any amount of clarity they can find in a crazy, mixed-up world.

We do the best we can with what we have been given. We succeed. We fail. We grow. We regress. We build positive relationships in our lives only to see others fall to the wayside. Life has an ebb and flow of comfort and confusion, but despite all that we experience and learn, life without Christ is like trying to do a connect-the-dots exercise without any numbers. We try to navigate the dots using our experience to help us gain a better understanding of the big picture. Or perhaps even more common, we let the world tell us what the picture is supposed to look like. Friends, let me tell you, there is no better way to lose your identity than letting others shape your desires, your definition of success, or what it means to be happy. But even if you have learned to operate independent from the world's influence and you are shaping your own identity, it still doesn't matter what you have learned, what material wealth you have gained, or how good of you person you are, your life will never take shape or have direction like it will when you find your identity in Christ.

The purpose of the Connect the Dots curriculum is to show you how discovering God's will for your life will give you an entirely new outlook on who you are and what you are called to do, but I think it also illustrates the quote that "God doesn't call the qualified, He qualifies the called." The Bible is full of people, people just like you and me, who were broken. They had their own individual circumstances and limitations, but because they were willing to let God use them, they were able to use their brokenness to achieve

great things in the name of God. The deliverance of an entire race from slavery, defeating a giant, consulting with kings, prophecy: these types of miracles didn't only happen in Bible times. God is using His people even today to do huge, miraculous works. The enemy will try and convince you that you aren't worthy, that your stutter will get in the way of your speaking, that you're too small to overcome that giant in your life, or that you don't possess the wisdom to give anyone advice. But this is the truth: the larger your wounds are the greater God is glorified through your healing. The more broken you are the bigger the impact your testimony will have. When you find your identity in Christ, when you let go of what you want the picture to look like and trust God to connect the dots, He will use every one of your scars – spiritual, emotional, and physical – to affect real change in the lives of the others and to give them hope!

The
Journey
Principles™
YOUR JOURNEY, GOD'S PRINCIPLES

DANIEL

Perseverance

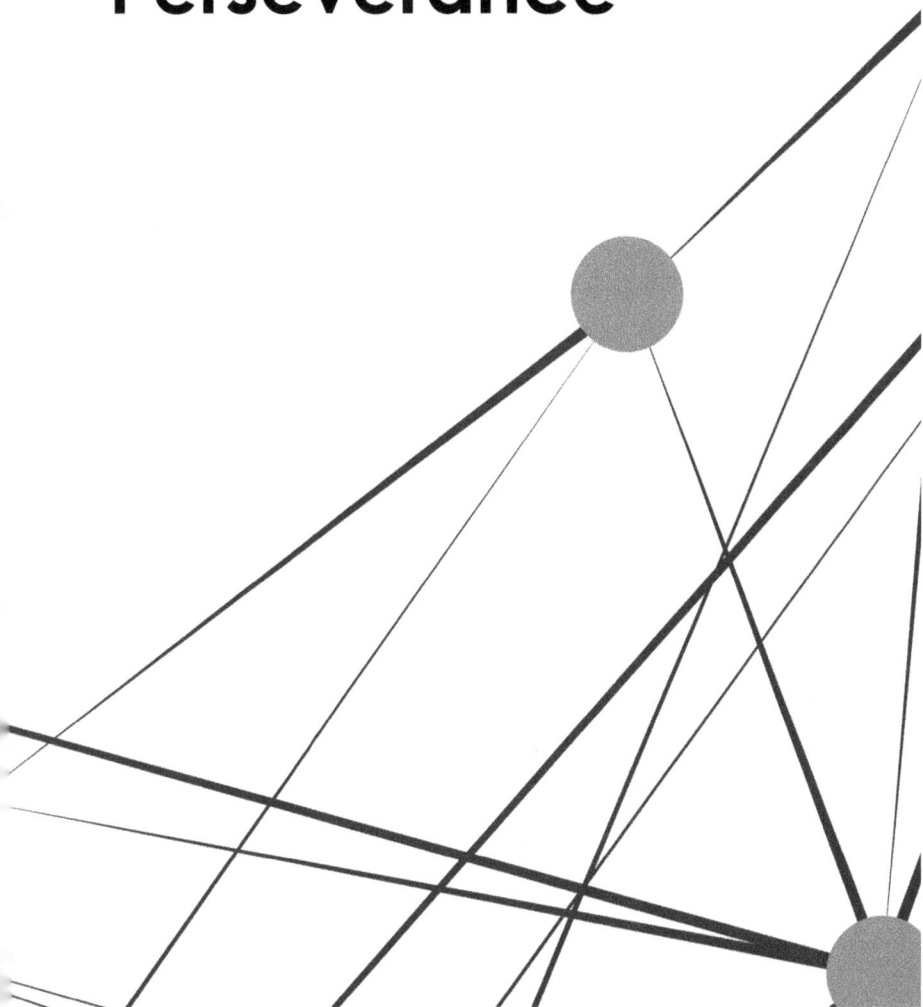

Ice-breaker Question:

Describe a time in your life when you stood up for something or someone.

Video Clip: Follow along questions for video (fill in the blank)

1. Daniel and his friends were _____ from their hometown and forced to live a _____ life.

2. The Babylonian lifestyle said that Daniel needed to _____ a certain way, talk a certain way, and _____ certain foods.

3. Daniel said that he wasn't created for a Babylonian lifestyle, but that he was created to _____ God. So Daniel resolved to fast for _____, faith, and _____.

4. Pastor Ed talked about a time in his life when he was deemed as an outcast or _____, but he knew that God had great plans and _____ for his life and now he is pastoring a life-giving church.

5. When Daniel defined his belief system there was nothing that could _____ his foundation.

6. People today don't want you to _____. People today don't want Christians to have resolve. What they want to see is believers who are shaken and who _____ to the world and culture of today. But like Daniel we need to have great resolve and perseverance!

Group Questions and Exercises:

1. Read the first chapter of Daniel and list the things that happened to Daniel, Shadrach, Meshach, and Abednego. What were they asked to change?

2. Now read the first three words of verse 8 to reveal the JP takeaway for this section. Can you think of a time when you compromised your faith (peer pressure, a boss, etc.)? Or a time when you showed resolve and stood firm in your faith? Share the circumstances of one experience and what you learned.

3. What do the following verses teach us about resolve/perseverance? 2 Peter 1:5-7, Philippians 3:14, James 1:2-5, James 1:12, 2 Chronicles 15:7, 1 Corinthians 13:7

4. Read chapter 2 verses 1-16. If what stood between you and life or death was the interpretation of a dream, what would you pray for? I think most of us would ask God to interpret the dream for us, right?!? But that's not what Daniel does. Read verses 17 and 18. What does Daniel ask his friends to pray for? What does this prayer teach us about how we should approach God?

5. Read Daniel 6:3-4. What if a government agency decided to look into your affairs? What would they find if they looked at your DVR, your internet history, or taped conversations of you with the guys or girls around the watercooler or out to lunch? Individually, not with any group members, but just by yourself, take a piece of paper and write down an area of your life that you know you need to submit to God.

Prayer Directive:

If you read the entire book of Daniel one thing that is evident is the power of prayer! We see Daniel pray a lot, but with big issues such as possibly facing death, the first thing Daniel does is take the prayer request to his friends (Daniel 2:17-18). Each one of you wrote down something that you needed to give to the Lord. Most likely each of you wrote down something different, but you are all united in your need. Pray over each other as you each begin this journey of submission. Your paths are unique, but your enemy and your desired destination are the same. Support each other in your journeys even if the need remains private and unspoken.

NOTE: *(JP Clydesdales quote?) No one is asking you to share what you wrote down if you don't want to, but working through an obstacle by yourself is so much harder than sharing the burden with a support group. It doesn't have to be someone in group, but it is recommended that you find someone to share the load (physically, emotionally, and spiritually). Reread the action steps for faithfulness in Ruth's section paying special attention to step 2.*

JP Takeaway: Journey Principle and Action Steps:

	DEFINE	ALIGN	SHINE
DANIEL RESOLVE/ PERSEVERANCE	You will be moved from a shaky foundation. Define your belief system. Know exactly who you are, what you believe, and why you believe it! He only is my rock and my salvation, My stronghold; I shall not be greatly shaken (Psalm 62:2).	Align your actions with your beliefs. You can talk all you want, but you will be known by your fruits. When the time comes for someone to question your character, do not give them any ammunition. Remember, when they went after Daniel, they "could find no corruption in him."	Having found your identity in Christ, knowing His word, and walking in His will, let Him shine through you in every way. And whatever you do, whether in word or deed, do it all in the name of the Lord Jesus, giving thanks to God the Father through him (Colossians 3:17).

Notes

_____

_____

_____

_____

_____

_____

_____

_____

_____

_____

_____

_____

_____

_____

_____

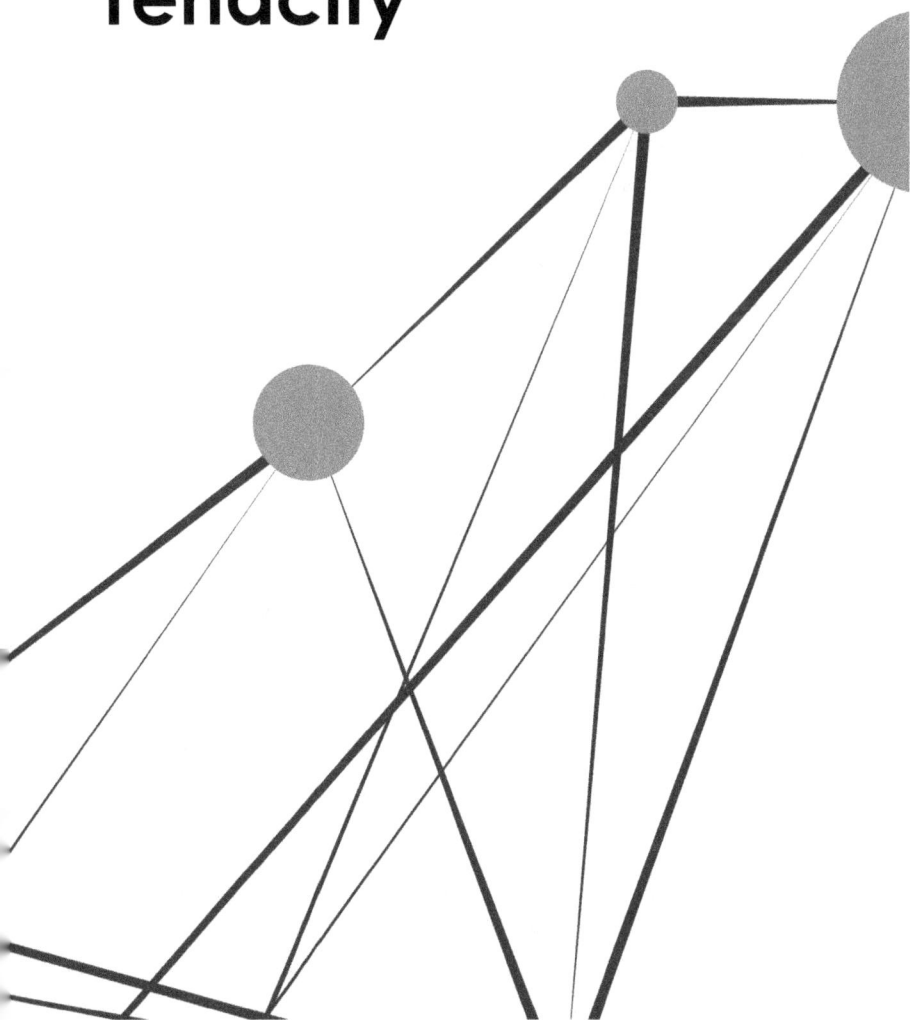

JACOB

Tenacity

Ice-breaker Question:

Describe a time in your life when you had to fight for something or someone. Looking back, how do you feel about the way things happened and the outcome?

Video Clip: Follow along questions for video (fill in the blank)

1. Jacob and Esau had a sibling rivalry. The Bible even tells us that they _____ in the womb.

2. Esau traded Jacob his birthright for a bowl of _____.

3. Jacob worked seven years for Rachel's hand in marriage, but was tricked into working _____ years.

4. Synonyms for tenacity are _____, perseverance, or _____.

5. Part of organization is knowing your resources. In every-day life, knowing your resources is as simple as knowing your _____ and your _____.

6. The opposite of tenacity is _____ or indifference. Choosing indifference is the same thing as not choosing _____.

Group Questions and Exercises:

1. Jacob was devious and untrustworthy. Esau was impulsive and shortsighted. I don't think anyone would want to be compared to either of these brothers in their adolescence, but if you had to choose, which would you say you are most like and why?

2. Think about what Jacob was trying to accomplish by obtaining Esau's birthright and then think about where it landed him – working for his Uncle Laban. What is so ironic about Jacob's change in circumstances?

3. Think back to a time in your life when it seemed like God had a sense of humor. Describe a circumstance when He used irony to better help you understand something He was teaching you.

4. Has there ever been a time when you wrestled with God. Were you as persistent as Jacob or were you quickly put in your place? What did you learn about yourself? What did you learn about God? What if I told you that God wants us to wrestle with Him? God wants us to be obedient to his commands, but He knows that in our finite humanness that we will very often not understand His plans. Think of your prayer life as stepping onto the mat with God. He wants to reveal Himself to you, but part of your growth is learning how to be receptive. When you spar with God, He will teach you how to move beyond just throwing jabs, surface questions that don't really hit at the meat of the issue or self-centered demands that merely seek relief rather than growth.

5. There are two types of stubbornness – there is prideful stubbornness that has no objective, but is stubborn for stubbornness sake, and then there is the type of stubbornness that is a clear display of strength in the face of conflict. That type of stubbornness is often referred to as tenacity or resolve.

   A. Take a moment and think about someone who you consider to be a great historical figure that you both admire and respect because of the profound impact they had on the world. List three of their strengths, but do not use tenacity or resolve.

   B. The odds are that tenacity could have been used for the person who you chose, but you were asked not to use it because I want you to think about tenacity not as trait, but as a supplement to the other traits you listed. You see, world changers don't do anything half way; they do everything with tenacity! Mother Teresa had tenacious compassion. Aristotle tenaciously sought wisdom. Da Vinci had tenacious curiosity. Jesus loves you with a tenacity you will never be able to comprehend. He loves you so tenaciously He was willing to give His life for yours. Take a moment to meditate on His sacrifice then praise Him for the way He loves you!

Prayer Directive:

1. Think of the influence Rebekah had in Jacob's life. Is there someone in your life who isn't a good influence? Ask God for power to stand strong in your faith and not be easily swayed. Pray that He would use you to be a positive influence in that person's life.

2. Wrestling with God should be a way to better understand yourself, what you should be learning through your current conflict or circumstances, the character of God, and His plan and purpose for you. The purpose of wrestling with God is to grow closer to Him, but

wrestling with God is not trying to barter or reason with Him. That's not how He works. Think about any ways you are trying approach God in this manner. Ask God to forgive you for your selfishness. Even if you can't fully understand His plan at the moment, go to Him. Wrestle with Him! Ask Him to help you better understand His design, but be prepared in case His answer is to be still and wait. If that is the case, ask Him for strength and patience to move forward in faith. He is your supply!

JP Takeaway: Journey Principle and Action Steps:

	VISUALIZE	ORGANIZE	ENERGIZE
JACOB **TENACITY** For some people, tenacity comes easy. They just have that "can do" attitude. For others, tenacity must be learned and it takes a great plan and encouragement to keep them pushing forward.	Dream! Dream big!!! There is nothing wrong with having big dreams. If you are earnestly trying to walk in the Spirit, then God will show you which dreams are worthy of pursuit, but they have to start with a vision.	Map out the steps to your goal, but be adaptive. Have a plan, but don't worry when it becomes necessary to amend or change it. Know your resources! This may include finances, but in everyday life it is as simple as knowing your strengths and surrounding yourself with the right support group to compliment your weaknesses. Making "mini goals" as steps toward your vision is less daunting and completing each step gives encouragement to press forward to the next step.	Energizing isn't just about putting your plans into action; it's about adopting the right attitude to keep your plans in motion. Conflict is inevitable, but being able to keep a positive attitude through the struggles is what will keep dreams from dying.

Notes

_____

_____

_____

_____

_____

_____

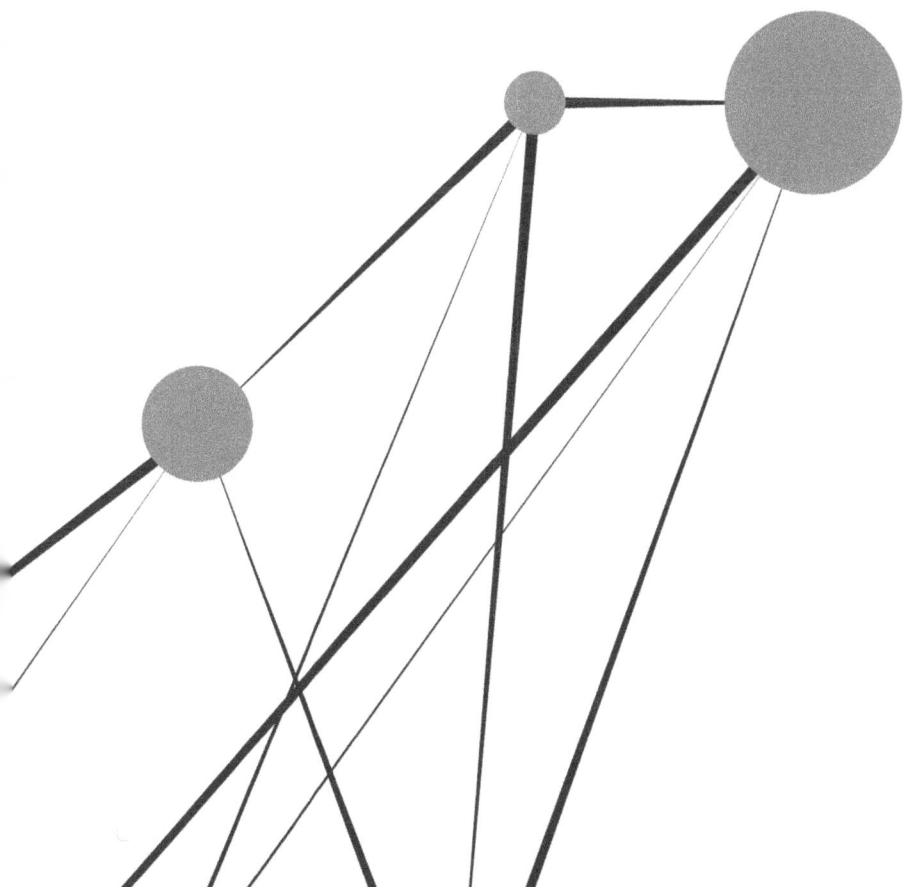

DAVID

Repentance

Ice-breaker Question:

Has there ever been a time in your life when you were completely humiliated? Has there been a time when you were humbled? What's the difference between the two?

IVideo Clip: Follow along questions for video (fill in the blank)

1. David was a musician and poet. He was also called a man of _____ by Saul's servants. He was a giant-slayer. He became _____. He was known as a _____.

2. David was also an adulterer and a _____.

3. Yet, David is still known as a man after _____ _____ _____.

4. When you look at _____ from a Biblical perspective, you can see that it is the one way we can get to God's heart.

5. What are the three practical ways to exercise the muscle of repentance? Review, _____, and _____.

Group Questions and Exercises:

1. Read 1 Samuel 17. The story of David and Goliath is probably one of the best-known stories in the Bible. Have you overcome a "giant" in your life? Maybe it has been a toxic relationship, addiction, or disease. Share how God helped you in your battle. Maybe you are still in the midst of war. If you feel comfortable, share your "giant" with your group so that your brothers and sisters can unite with you in prayer.

2. Even though Saul was hunting David, there were two different times that David could have killed Saul (1 Samuel 24 and 26). David respected and obeyed God's will even though killing Saul would have solved all of David's problems. Can you think of a time when you chose the easy path instead the right one? In hindsight, how do you feel about the decision? Has there been a time where you chose the right path instead of the easy one? What did you learn?

3. One of the reasons that David is described as "a man after God's heart" is because of his passion. However, the difference between a trait being good or bad is simply whether it is being used to serve God and advance His kingdom or whether it is being used to serve yourself and advance your own selfish desires. David was passionate, but he was passionate about doing what was right! Think about a trait in your life that has been both good and bad. What can you do to keep that trait focused in the right direction and let it be a strength and not a weakness?

4. "A man after God's own heart" – For some that title is difficult to understand since David was an adulterer and a murderer. It's true, David made some huge mistakes in his life, but no matter the size of his transgressions, David was always repentant! When the prophet Nathan confronted David about his adultery with Bathsheba, David cried out "I have sinned against the Lord!" Then, David wrote one of the most beautiful and touching songs, Psalms 51. Is there a transgression that you haven't yet given to the Lord? Repent! Go to Psalms 51. Take a sheet of paper and write down the sin for which you need to ask forgiveness from the Lord. Beneath it, rewrite verses 1-17 in your own words and make that your prayer to God today!

5. David gave us clues in his own writings to other traits that describe a man after God's own heart. Read the verses below and write down the trait you think each verse is describing.
Psalm 18:1, Psalm 18:3, Psalm 27:1, Psalm 119:34, Psalm 9:1

Prayer Directive:

Pray: Father, thank you for taking the time to knit me in the womb, thank you for knowing how many hairs are on my head, and thank you that in your perfect love you chose to send your Son to give His life in ransom for my own. Oh God, thank you that because of His sacrifice, when you look at me you don't see my sins, but you see His flawlessness. Like David, I was born into sin and despite my best intentions I know that I fail you daily. But like David let me remain humble in your sight and have a heart that seeks you. Let me recognize my transgressions and turn from them quickly, confessing and repenting in your name. Give me strength to overcome the temptations of this world, all that's temporary and will give way. Let my heart remain in you, focused on your kingdom and all that is eternal.

JP Takeaway: Journey Principles and Action Steps:

	REVIEW	RENOUNCE	RENEW
DAVID REPENTANCE	Realize that you have done wrong and take responsibility for your actions.	Renounce can mean to reject, but it can also mean to surrender. Turning away from your sin is important, but giving it to God is much more important. David says in Psalms to "cast all of your cares on the Lord and He will sustain you." To cast means to fling or hurl and when you throw something with force it is no longer beside you where it can easily be picked back up.	Attempt to make amends for your trespasses. You must try to restore the relationships that have been fractured or broken. Forgiveness from that person(s) is not up to you, but taking the proper steps to give them the opportunity to forgive you is in your control and is an integral step in moving past guilt and shame. But beyond any earthly relationship, you must reconcile your relationship with God!

Notes

_____

_____

_____

_____

_____

_____

_____

_____

_____

_____

_____

_____

_____

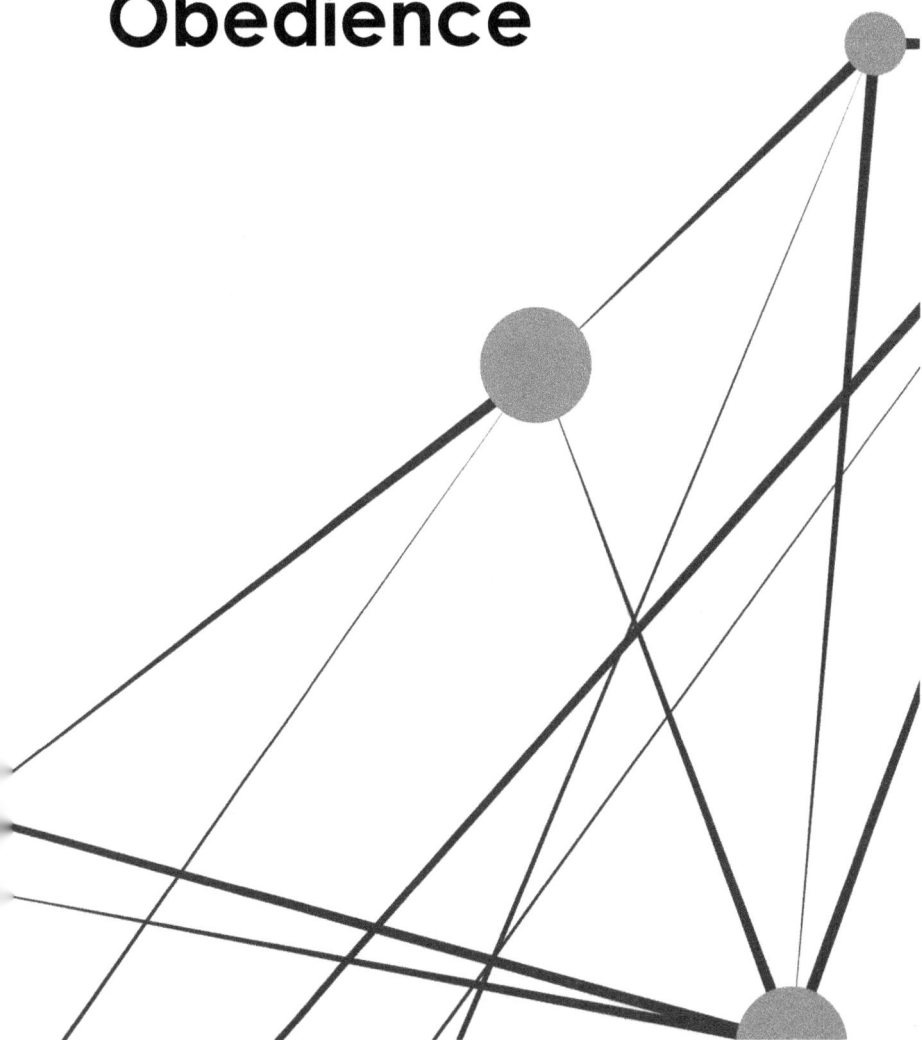

ABRAHAM

Obedience

Ice-breaker Question (before video):

Is there something in your life that would be very difficult for you to give up? Maybe it's coffee, a particular TV show, or maybe a social media site. Describe that one thing that would be hard to let go and why. What if God asked you to give it to Him?

Video Clip: Follow along questions for video (fill in the blank)

1. Dr. Sam heard God saying, "You have to speak up. I'll _____ _____ the words, but you have to at least start…and be _____."

2. When you are obedient. When you actually do what God wants you to do. You will be amazed at how God equips you with the _____ to do it.

3. Abraham was asked to do something that was very _____ and against his _____.

4. What separates the Christian from the non-Christian? Jesus says, "If you _____ me, you will _____ me."

5. In the Old Testament, God tells us that obedience is better than _____.

Group Questions and Exercises:

1. Think back to how you responded to the "ice-breaker" question at the beginning of the section. Has your perspective changed at all after reading about Abraham's obedience to God and his willingness to sacrifice Isaac?

2. Read Genesis 16:1-5. Think about a time in your life when you did something to please someone you cared about even though you knew it was a bad decision (Abraham's perspective). Or, has there been a time when you made a decision thinking it was what you wanted only to find great disappointment in the end? (Sarai's perspective)

3. Abraham and Sarai did not believe that they could have children at the ages of 100 and 90, but God blessed them with Isaac. Have you ever seen a miracle take place in your life or in the life of someone you know?

4. How does the story of Abraham taking Isaac to be sacrificed foreshadow the story of Jesus Christ? What are the symbolic parallels? Do you know the historical significance Mount Moriah (2 Samuel 24:18-25 and 2 Chronicles 3:1)? What is the modern day significance of Mount Moriah?

5. What do the following verses teach about being obedient to God? What do they show us about God's character? Or, describe the "call to action" or directions given.
John 15:9, Romans 1:5, Hebrews 13:17, John 14:15, 2 John 1:6, Luke 11:28, 1 Peter 1:14

Prayer Directive:

Pray: Most high God, You tell me that if I love you, I will keep your commands. Let the world look upon my life and never question how much I love you! Give me patience to wait on you. Let me become so familiar with your voice that I can recognize any imposter. Give me strength to follow through with your instruction to the end no matter what arrows the enemy throws in my direction. I know you love me. Because you love me I will trust in you and remain obedient. I commit myself and my family to you Lord God. We will seek to honor and glorify you in all that we do and let this act of worship be pleasing in your sight.

JP Takeaway: Journey Principle and Action Steps:

	ADMIT	EQUIP	SUBMIT
ABRAHAM OBEDIENCE	Confess that you have been trying to do things on your own instead of listening for God's voice. Admit that His ways are better than your own.	Arm yourself with the Word of God! Know His promises to you. (Jeremiah 29:11, 2 Peter 1:4, Isaiah 40:29-31, etc.)	Make His will for your life your only priority. Learn to discern the difference between your own wants/desires and trust Him to meet your needs. He is your supply!

Notes

_____

_____

_____

_____

_____

_____

_____

_____

_____

_____

_____

_____

_____

_____

_____

_____

_____

_____

_____

lesson 5

JOHN

Love

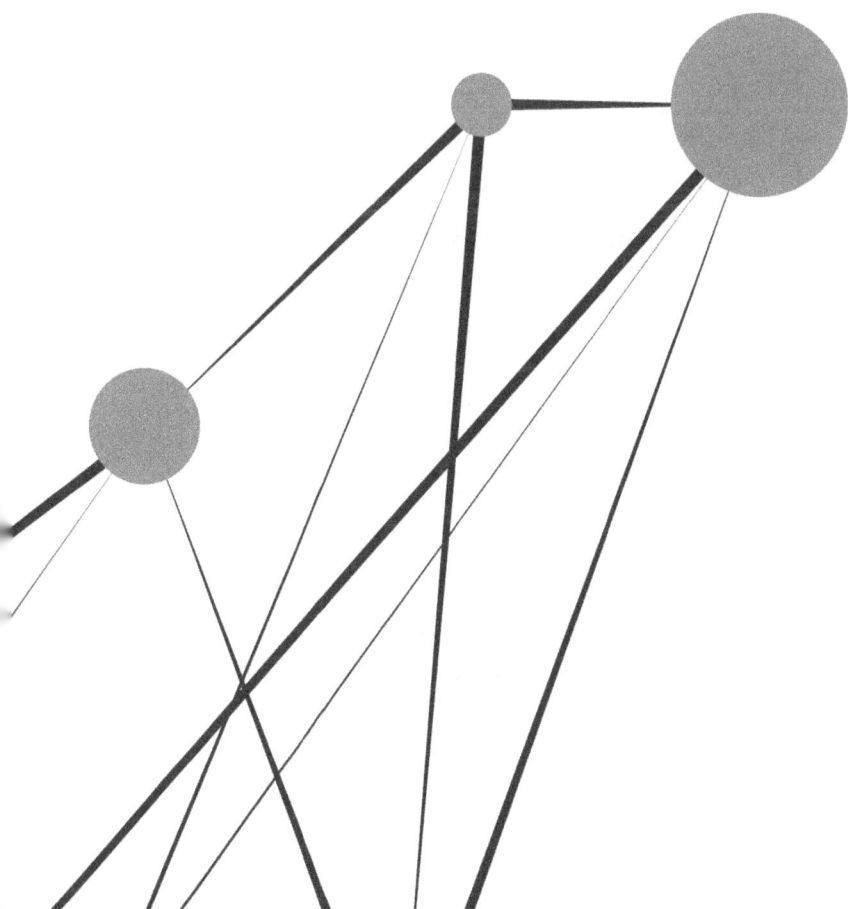

Ice-breaker Question:

Have you ever leapt before you looked or spoke before thinking? Talk about a time in your life when you acted/spoke too quickly.

Video Clip: Follow along questions for video (fill in the blank)

1. John was known as the one that _____ loved and as the apostle of _____.

2. The Gospel of John is the only Gospel that tells the story of Jesus _____ the disciple's feet.

3. Love and _____ cannot occupy the same space.

4. Life is full of _____. It is built on _____. We have to present, mindful, and _____ in every moment.

5. Love isn't _____; it's dynamic. Jesus' love for us was dynamic!

Group Questions and Exercises:

1. The Gospels, the books of Matthew, Mark, Luke, and John have a lot of overlapping content, but the different perspectives give insight to the unique characters of each apostle. The book of John, however, is the only Gospel that tells the story of Jesus washing the disciple's feet at the last supper. How do you think that experience impacted John's life? Read John 13:1-17. How many character traits of Jesus can you list from this one event?

2. John is often referred to as "the apostle of love" and actually refers to himself in his own writings as "the one who Jesus loved." We can glean from his narrative that he did truly love the people with whom he came into contact, but we also see that he had a passion for truth. When John was critical in his writing it was most often about those who would pervert the truth (read 1 John 2:3-6). Share and discuss your viewpoints on truth and love. What are the dynamics of their relationship?

3. Read John 19:25-27. What does it say about John for Jesus to entrust His mother into John's care?

4. Read the following verses that John wrote about love. What do they teach us about God?
John 3:16, 15:13; 1 John 4:8, 4:18-19, 3:16-19, 4:7

5. Most of the apostles had successful ministries after Jesus' resurrection, but all of them were martyred except for John. However, while he didn't experience a violent death, he was exiled to the island of Patmos in his late eighties or early nineties. Put yourself in John's shoes for a moment. Think about everything he got to experience. John was in a select group with James and Peter who got to experience Jesus in ways that the others couldn't even imagine, but even within that select group, Jesus considered John to be His best friend. How cool is that?!? And yet after everything John had seen and done, he outlived Jesus and every other apostle and, at a very old age, was left alone on an island where he must have believed he would die. What would you be feeling at that moment? What type of thoughts would be running through your mind? What questions would you have for God? But the most amazing thing happened to John. At a time when he was most likely about to give up all hope, God spoke to John and gave him the book of Revelation. What does that say about God's plans for us? What can we learn about looking outside of life's circumstances and continuing, no matter what, to be an open vessel for God's amazing works?

Prayer Directive:

Pray: Lord Jesus, thank you for your truth, but above all thank you for your love! Give me a passion to seek your wisdom. Let me search for your face in all that I see and do. Help me to recognize the ways that you exhibit grace and mercy in my life and, for the innumerable ways that I am blessed that I know will never see Father, I give you praise for your amazing protection and provision. Lord, in all the ways that I want to grow closer to you, that I want to know you more, please never let me lose sight of how I am commanded to love and show compassion in your truth. Never let me get so focused on being right in your name that I disgrace it by not showing your love. Amen.

JP Takeaway: Journey Principle and Action Steps:

	PATIENCE	KINDNESS	HUMILITY
JOHN **LOVE**	Proverbs 16:32 – Better a patient person than a warrior, one with self-control than one who takes a city.	Ephesians 4:32 – Be kind to one another, tender-hearted, forgiving each other, just as God in Christ also has forgiven you.	Mark 9:35 – Sitting down, Jesus called the Twelve and said, "Anyone who wants to be first must be the very last, and he servant of all." Note: look back to Aaron's section and the three specific action steps for humility.

Notes

_____

_____

_____

_____

_____

_____

_____

_____

_____

_____

_____

_____

_____

_____

_____

_____

_____

_____

lesson 6

RUTH

Faithfulness

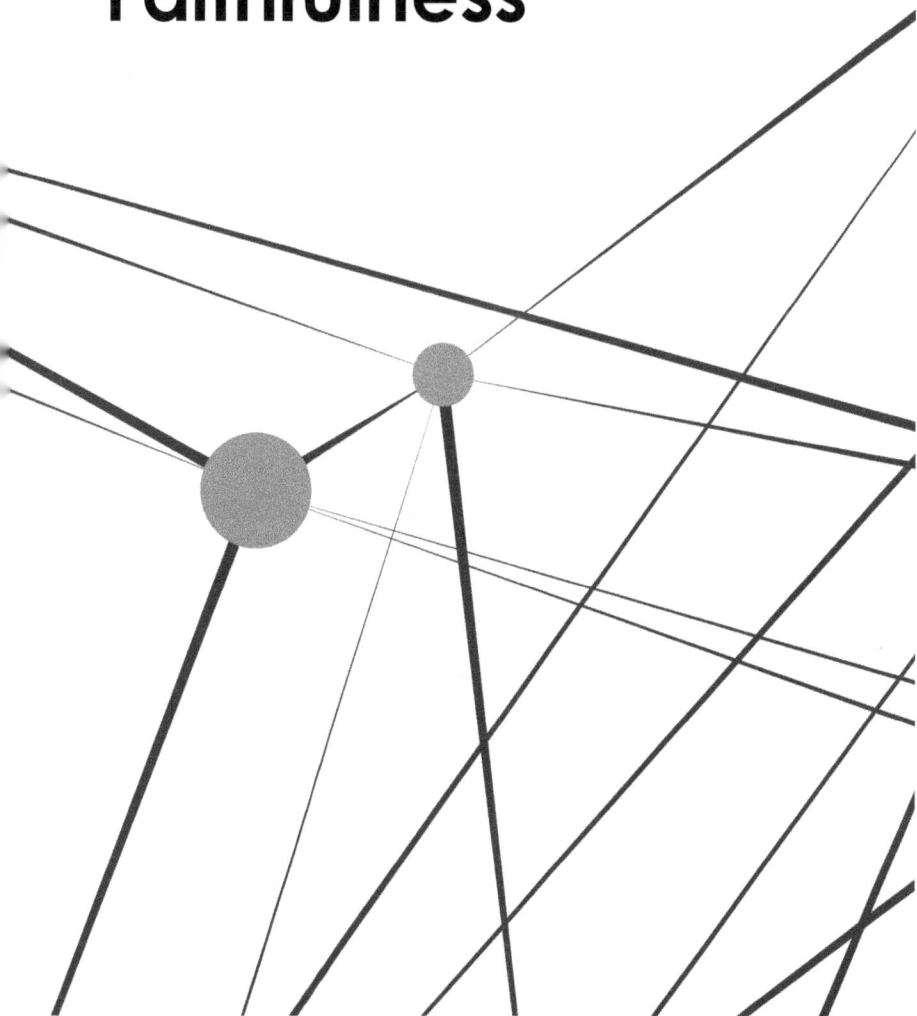

Ice-breaker Question:

Think of a time in your life where you had to patient. Describe what it was that you were forced to wait on, describe the anticipation, and was it worth the wait. What did you learn from this experience?

Video Clip: Follow along questions for video (fill in the blank)

1. Ruth was married, but lost her _____ before she had any _____.

2. Ruth accompanied Naomi to her homeland where she met and married _____.

3. The first action step for faithfulness is to _____ God's plan.

4. Declaring your choice to someone else creates _____.

Group Questions and Exercises:

1. Read Ruth 1:1-17. Put yourself in Ruth's shoes. In one direction is your family and the only home you have ever known and, in the other, complete mystery. Which would you have chosen? What does this say about Ruth?

2. What do these verses teach us about Ruth's character? List 3 strengths.

3. Read Ruth 3. Verse 11 says that all the people of the town knew Ruth was a woman of noble character," but in what ways does this chapter describe the nobility of Boaz?

4. At the end of Ruth 4, we are told the significance of Ruth's posterity. What a story of redemption! You might say that redemption runs in her family tree, especially since her bloodline leads to Jesus Christ, The Redeemer Himself, but there is also another story of redemption in Ruth's ancestry. Discuss the similarities between the story of Ruth and the story of her mother-in-law. Hint: Salmon, Boaz's father was a spy in Jericho.

5. What do the following verses teach about faithfulness or in what ways do they instruct on how to be faithful?
Proverbs 3:5, Ephesians 2:8, Luke 16:10, Deuteronomy 6:5, Proverbs 28:20

Prayer Directive:

Pray: Father God, faithfulness is a gift that comes from you, so help me to trust in You Lord and lean not on my understanding. When the world, my flesh, or my intellect tells me take one path, make your direction known to me. Even if I don't yet understand your will Father, give me the faith to move in confidence knowing that you have gone before me to light my way. Your ways are good oh God! They are so much more complete than any wish or desire that I have for myself. When conflict comes Lord, don't let me question your course, let me delight in the struggle that would refine my faith and bring me closer to you.

JP Takeaway: Journey Principle and Action Steps:

	DETERMINE	DECLARE	DEVOTE
RUTH **FAITHFULNESS**	Discern God's voice and determine His will for you! The Bible says that Satan disguises himself as an angel of light, so remaining faithful isn't just about finding a good plan, it's about finding the right plan – God's plan!	Make your choice known. It's not necessary to share all of your decisions with everyone in the world, but you should have accountability partners in your life. If you do not make a declaration, the enemy will use your silence against you. When you are tempted it will come with the thought, "well I didn't tell anyone so it won't hurt to change my mind or not stick with it." Confess and set yourself up for success.	Commit yourself to your choice! It sounds so easy, but we are so easily distracted. If you find that you are having trouble staying devoted, try setting up a commitment schedule. Instead of thinking of your commitment as a single long-term choice, think of it as a daily re-commitment. Pray for focus, strength, and patience – whatever it is that you need to achieve your goal – and let that prayer change and grow each new day. If daily doesn't work, do multiple times a day (maybe around meals) until it sticks.

Notes

_____

_____

_____

_____

_____

_____

_____

_____

_____

_____

_____

_____

_____

ELIJAH

Selflessness

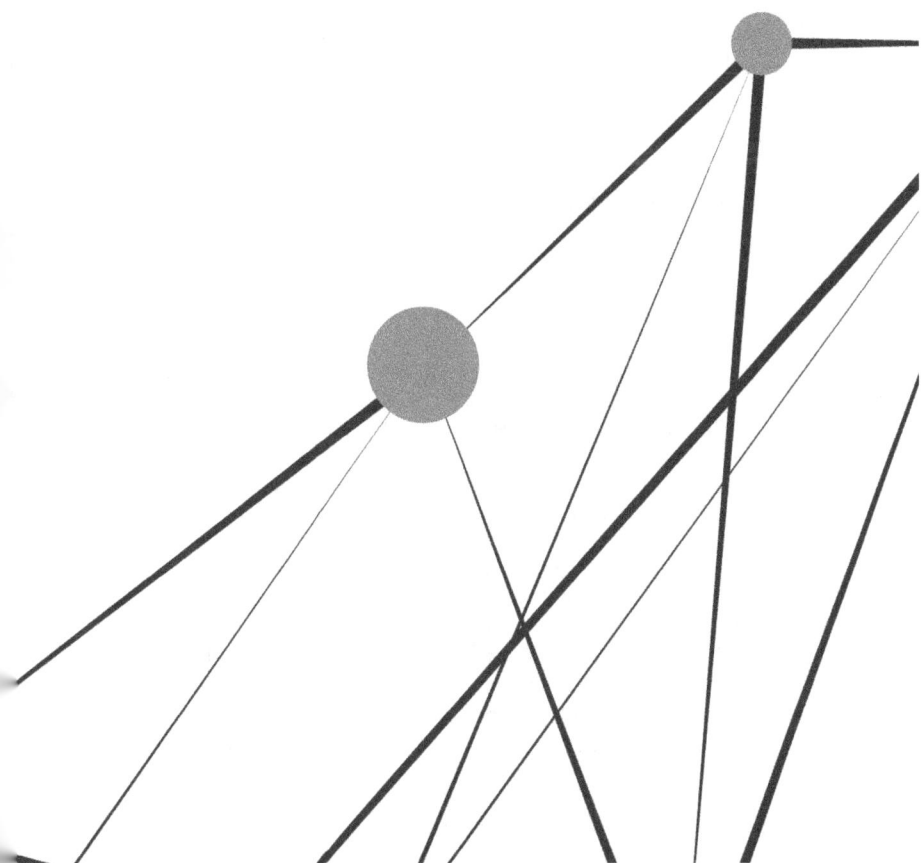

Ice-breaker Question:

Would you consider yourself an introvert or an extrovert? How do large groups or crowds affect you? How do you feel when you are alone? What environments take or recharge your energy?

Video Clip: Follow along questions for video (fill in the blank)

1. Elijah, like so many of us, experienced things in his life like _____, depression, and _____.

2. The widow heeded the warning of Elijah and because of her _____ she was not in need when the famine came.

3. Karen experienced victory when she moved past her own agenda and opened herself up to the strengths and _____ that God gave her.

4. Forget about the _____ the world tells you that you need to be successful. Instead pour into the _____ in your life.

Group Questions and Exercises:

1. We first meet Elijah in 1 Kings 17 when he warns King Ahab of a great drought. Read verses 2-6. What is the first character trait we see in Elijah? What is God's response to this trait?

2. The rest of chapter 17 describes how God multiplied the flour and oil for the widow at Zarephath because of her willingness to help Elijah. Can you think about a time when God blessed you through multiplication? Maybe it was also with food or maybe a time when it seemed like there wasn't enough money for your bills, but when it came time to pay them the money was there. Share your testimony.

3. Elijah is a character that many people find relatable. He had his ups and his downs. He had moments where he stood resolute in God's strength and those where he fled in fear like when Jezebel threatened his life. Elijah was so anxious and afraid that he told the Lord that he had enough and asked God to take his life. Not everyone has reached a point in their life where they contemplated suicide, but maybe there was a time when you felt spiritually

hollow, like you had lost your connection with God, or even like He had abandoned or betrayed you. This moment is often referred to as "The Dark Night of the Soul." It's not always easy to talk about, but sharing a moment like this will minister to someone else in your group. Describe what it was like to be in the middle of that experience, how you worked your way through it, and, most importantly, how God used that experience in your life to draw you closer to Him.

4. Elijah did some pretty amazing miracles in his day including bringing the widow at Zarephath's son back from the dead, but despite all of the incredible things that he did, Elijah always declared that he was doing it in the name of the Lord. That's humility! Read 1 Kings 18:25-29. Does Elijah sound humble in this passage? Discuss the differences between humility and being bold in the name of God. When does confidence become cockiness?

5. What do these verses teach about selfishness? (Romans 2:8, James 3:14-15, Philippians 2:3, Galatians 5:19-21). Read the following verses about selflessness and humility and answer the corresponding questions.

   • Where does selflessness/humility begin? (John 3:30, Galatians 2:20, John 5:30, Galatians 5:16-17)

   • What is the next level? (Mark 12:31, 1 Peter 3:8, Romans 12:10)

   • Does it end there? (Luke 6:27-28, Leviticus 19:18)

Prayer Directive:

Pray: Lord, there's a reason why you tell us about a path that is narrow and a path that is wide. Your way was not meant to be comfortable, but conflict initiates growth which brings us closer to you. Father, forgive me when I forget that. Forgive me when I lose sight of your purpose and plan and, in my flesh, become anxious or fearful. Like with Elijah, Lord, please continue to pursue me even when my world gets turned upside down and I somehow lose sight of your mercy and grace. Continue to speak to me, amongst the fire and the shifting of the earth, whisper your truth in my ear and let me rest in your good and perfect peace.

JP Takeaway: Journey Principle and Action Steps:

	ZOOM OUT	BROOM OUT	GROOM OUT
ELIJAH SELFLESSNESS	It's so easy to become preoccupied with all the little things that the world tells us we need to be happy. Take a step back from the distractions that create selfishness in your life, look at the big picture, and take inventory of the things that truly matter to you. Hint: your list should have people's names on it and NOT stuff!	Now that you have taken inventory, clean out the clutter! Remove the idols that you have created in your life that sidetrack you from submitting fully to God's will and keep you from becoming the best version of you who can truly impact the world: in your marriage, as a parent, a friend, an employee, or in your church.	You've removed the distractions and you've figured out what is important to you; start pouring yourself into those relationships. Groom them; invest in them. It will start with those who are close to you, but it won't end there. When you learn to open your heart and invest in others, you will find yourself willing to go out of your way for someone you may not even know.

Notes

_____

_____

_____

_____

_____

_____

_____

_____

_____

_____

_____

_____

_____

_____

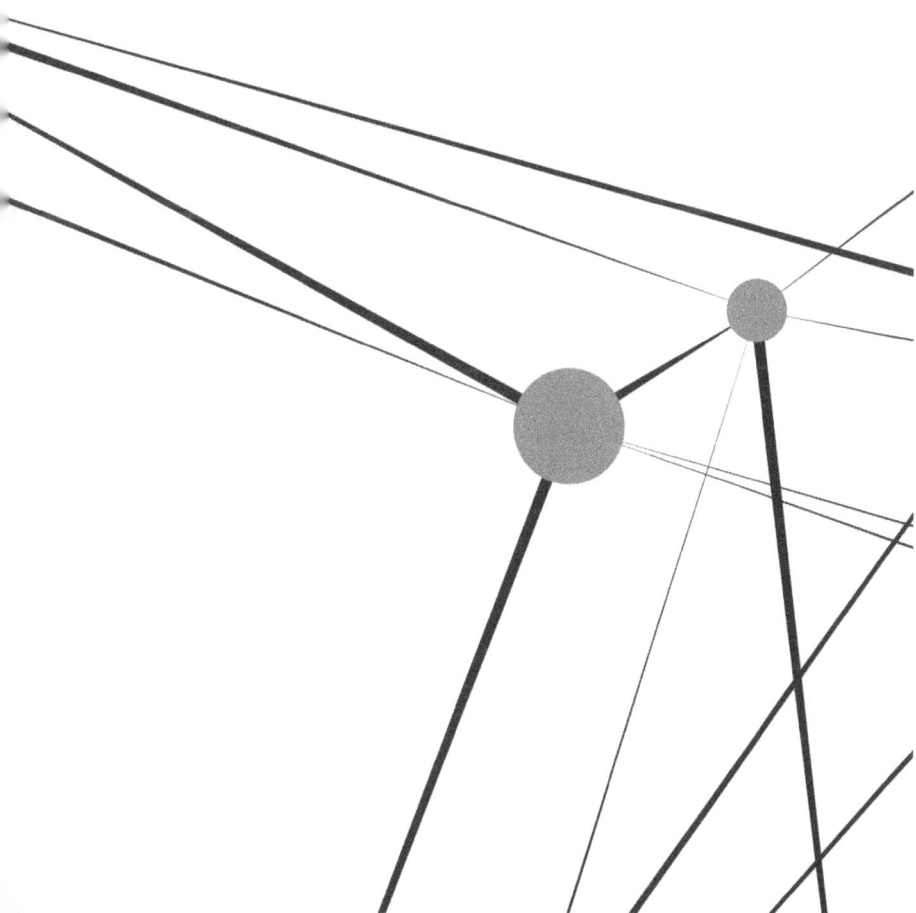

JONATHAN

Loyalty

Ice-breaker Question:

What is the most courageous thing you have ever done? What motivated you to overcome the fear/anxiety?

Video Clip: Follow along questions for video (fill in the blank)

1. Jonathan shows his _____ to God's will by committing himself to David. He gives David his robe, his _____, and his _____.

2. Jonathan makes a _____ with David and says, "_____ you want I will do."

3. Saul continually tried to _____ David, but Jonathan always stood in the _____.

4. The foundation of loyalty is _____.

5. The stronger the _____ of a relationship is, the more _____ the relationship becomes.

Group Questions and Exercises:

1. Read 1 Samuel 14. Would you describe Jonathan's actions as foolish or courageous? If you were Jonathan's armor-bearer, would you have followed Jonathan? The passage says that God "shook the ground."

2. Do you think that the earthquake was a response to Jonathan's faith that God would act on his behalf? Have you seen an "earthquake" happen in your life or the life of someone you know? Share that story with the group.

3. By the time we get to 1 Samuel 18, we have seen David's anointing and he has slain Goliath. Then we are told that "Jonathan became one in spirit with David, and he loved him as himself...and Jonathan made a covenant with David because he loved him as himself. Jonathan took off the robe he was wearing and gave it to David, along with his tunic, and even his sword, his bow and his belt." Have you ever had this type of friendship in your life? If so, who are you in the relationship, David or Jonathan?

4. What do the following verses tell us about Jonathan's character?
1 Samuel 18:1-3, 19:2, 20:4, 20:16, 20:30-33, 20:42

5. What do the following verses tell us about the importance of friendship, how to be a good friend, or what type of relationships to avoid?
Proverbs 17:17, 12:26, 13:20, John 15:13, Ecclesiastes 4:9-10, Proverbs 27:17, 22:24-25, 12:26

Prayer Directive:

If the Lord has blessed you with a friendship like the one we see between Jonathan and David, praise Him for the amazing blessing of a best friend who loves you and supports you unconditionally. If you don't have this type of relationship in your life, don't be afraid to ask your Father for this blessing and ask for guidance and wisdom in your search.

JP Takeaway: Journey Principle and Action Steps:

	HONESTY	DEPENDABILITY	DURABILITY
JONATHAN **LOYALTY**	The foundation of any relationship is trust and trust begins with honesty. It's that simple! Being open and real is what strengthens a relationship and allows it to grow.	Dependability isn't only about being there when you are needed, it also means being trustworthy, supportive, sincere, and dedicated.	The different definitions of durability say it all! 1. The state or quality of being durable and/or flexible 2. The power to endure through any condition 3. The ability to resist agents and influences that trigger change, decay, or dissolution

Notes

_____

_____

_____

_____

_____

_____

_____

_____

_____

_____

_____

_____

_____

_____

_____

_____

_____

RAHAB

Redemption

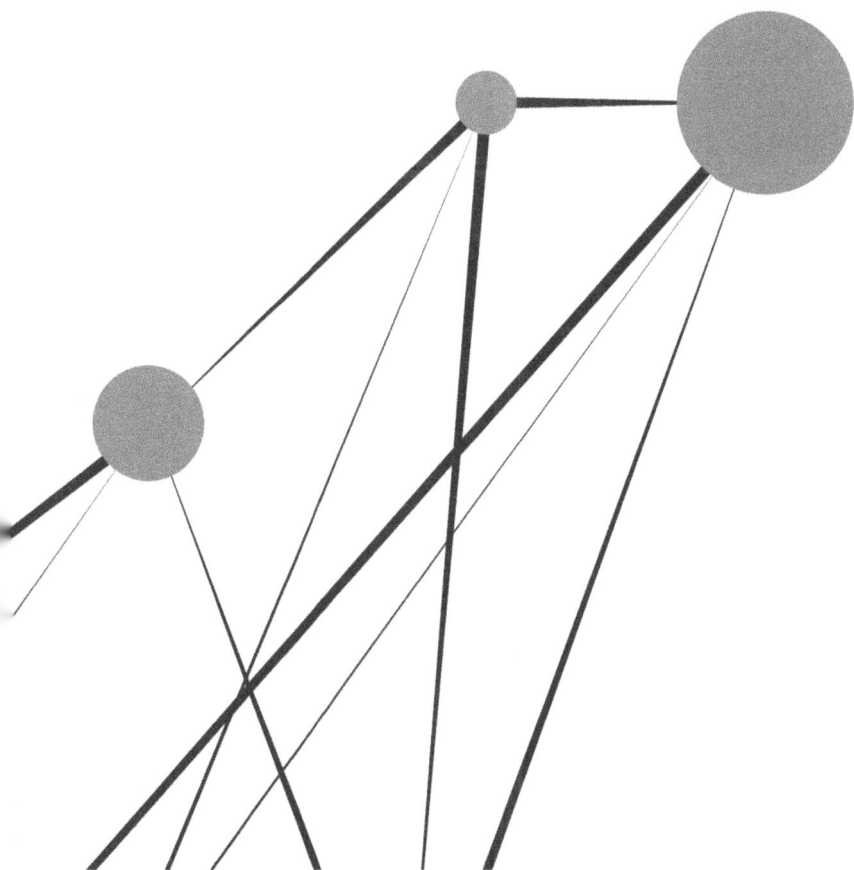

Ice-breaker Question:

On a scale from 1-10, 10 being the strongest, how would rate the strength of your faith and why? Where is it strongest? Where can it use the most growth?

Video Clip: Follow along questions for video (fill in the blank)

1. Rahab hid the two spies on the _____ of her _____.

2. Rahab asked the two spies that, since she had shown them _____, would they _____ to save her and her family since she knew that God had already given them the city.

3. The beautiful about Rahab is that she was an _____ person. She was a _____.

4. Many of us have areas in our life where we need _____, sins that we need to _____.

5. _____ heard Rahab when He turned to her that day. He saved her and _____.

Group Questions and Exercises:

1. 1.   Read Joshua 2, 6:17-25. Think about the story of Rahab. What three words would you use to describe her?

2. Talk about two areas in your life where you feel like your faith is the strongest and two where you believe that your faith could improve.

3. Describe a time when your trust was rewarded. Describe a time when it was betrayed.
   Do you know that both of those experiences were part of god's plan for your life? As much as it hurts to be betrayed, God uses even the most painful moments in our lives to draw us closer to Him, to teach us about His love. Deuteronomy 31:6 tells us to "be strong and courageous. Do not be afraid or terrified because of them, for the Lord your God goes with you; He will never leave you nor forsake you." (NIV) Our God is trustworthy and He is faithful!

4. The spies asked Rahab to put a scarlet cord out of her window so they would know which house was hers and that no one in it would be harmed much like the Passover that took place with Moses and the 10th plague of Egypt. Think about the significance of Passover? How does the importance of the original event translate into the story of Rahab?

5. Have different group members each look up one of the verses below and have them read it aloud to the group. Then, discuss what each verse teaches about trusting God.
   2 Samuel 7:28, Psalm 125:1, Proverbs 3:5-6, Psalm 9:10, Revelation 21:5

Prayer Directive:

Pray: Almighty God, you tell us in your word that faith is our shield! I want to learn to commit all of my life to you, to trust in your purpose and plan for my life. Thank you for the many ways in which you have rewarded my faith with blessings, and thank you for the mercy and grace you have shown even in the areas of my life where my faith is lacking. Draw me closer to you. Help me learn to better discern your voice Lord God. Make your works evident to me so that I can give you all the glory and rejoice in the richness and fullness of your will! I ask this in the name of Your Son, Jesus Christ!

JP Takeaway: Journey Principle and Action Steps

RAHAB REDEMPTION	CONFESS	BELIEVE	RECEIVE
If you have never accepted Christ as your savior and you would like to, please follow these simple steps. It will change your life forever! If you have accepted Christ and are looking for redemption in a personal matter, please refer to the Action Steps for "Repentance" in David's section.	Acknowledge that you are a sinner and that you want to repent of your sins.	Believe that Jesus Christ is the Son of God and that He was crucified and resurrected to pay the ransom for your sins.	Invite Jesus into your heart to be your personal Lord and savior. It's a free gift!

Notes

_____

_____

_____

_____

_____

_____

_____

_____

_____

_____

_____

_____

_____

_____

_____

_____

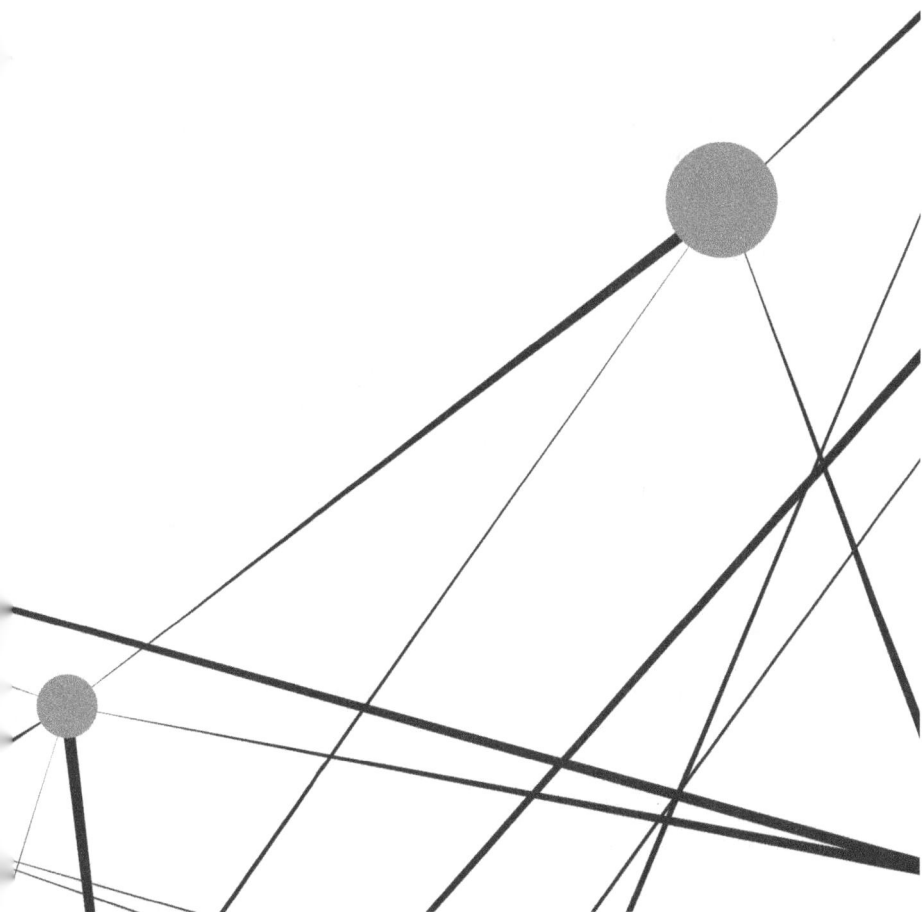

AARON

Humility

Ice-breaker Question:

Describe a time in your life where a very big need arose like a medical bill, a car breaking down, or your heat/AC going out, but God almost immediately provided a solution.

Video Clip: Follow along questions for video (fill in the blank)

1. Aaron was MOSES' older brother.

2. Aaron helped Moses hold up his _____ during battle so the Israelites could defeat the Amalekites.

3. Acts of _____ don't rot away; they stay in the heart forever.

4. Being easily _____ is a form of pride.

5. Humility doesn't mean that you think less of yourself; it means you think less _____ yourself.

6. A person of humility knows that their _____ comes from who they are in Christ.

Group Questions and Exercises:

1. Read Exodus 4:1-17. If you are like me, you may picture Charlton Hesston when you think about Moses, but the mighty Moses began his calling in fear – scared that a shepherd with a speech impediment couldn't be a messenger of God. Moses pleaded and begged God not to send him into Egypt, but when we first see Aaron, God tells us that "he is already on the way." What is your first impression of Moses? In the little you are given here, how would you contrast Aaron? What does this passage say about the character of god?

2. There's a quote that as far as I know is uncredited, but it says that "the best ability is availability." Can you describe an instance when simply being available led to a blessing in your life? Is there a moment in your life when it wasn't availability that brought you blessing, but a willingness to step up to the task when everyone else backed down?

3. Split up the verses below amongst the group. Read aloud and then discuss how the passages describe Aaron's strengths or how his actions aided Moses. Exodus 4:14-16, 7:10-13, 17:8-13, 24:13-14, 28:1-5, and Numbers 16:1-3. Now look up the following and describe the mistakes that Aaron made. Exodus 32:1-5, Numbers 12:1-15, 20:2-13. Think of the remarkable things that Aaron got to be a part of in his lifetime. He got to speak to pharaoh and play a significant role in the deliverance of his people from slavery. He held up Moses' arms in battle. He was the first priest of Israel. He developed a religious system that flourished for 1500 years. Yet, a few occurrences of listening to man instead of God or becoming angry and prideful and Aaron, along with Moses, was told that he would not see the Promised Land. ONE ACTION OR REACTION CAN CHANGE YOUR LIFE! Aaron slipped up. He made his mistakes. But how humbling is it to know that we serve a God of forgiveness! Psalm 103:12 tells us that "as far as the east is from the west, so far has He removed our transgressions from us." There is nothing we can do that the perfect love of our Father can't make new. Aaron must have repented of his sins·because we are told that he was consecrated to the Lord (Psalm 106) and that Israel mourned his death for 30 days (Numbers 20:29).

4. Is there a relationship in your life where you are Moses? Is there one where you are Aaron? You might only have one, but chances are you have both. Share with your group about the dynamics of these relationships and how God has brought you together to complement one another.

5. Aaron, for all his strengths, was easily swayed by others. Rather than standing firm in God's commands, he was tempted and swayed by the perceptions of man. Read Ephesians 6:10-20 and discuss what it really means to put on the full armor of God.

Prayer Directive:

Think about your willingness to serve. If you are called, will you plead like Moses that they find someone else or, like Aaron, will you already be on your way? Ask God to show you the areas in your life where you can be used to further His kingdom and ask Him to close the doors where you are wasting energy in tasks in which you have not been called.

JP Takeaway: Journey Principle and Action Steps:

	DETECT	REJECT	RESPECT
AARON HUMILITY/ SERVANT HEART	Examine yourself. Look for the areas in your life where you have trouble with pride or arrogance. Why do you think they exist and where did they come from?	Your journey is a pilgrimage to a better you. Don't let the enemy (Satan) or the world force you into a life of comparison with others or unhealthy expectations. Reject the lies and deceptions!	We are all fearfully and wonderfully made. We have unique personalities and spiritual gifts, but we are all God's creations. It is His will that we respect one another. (Philippians 2:3, Romans 12:10 Matthew 7:12)

Notes

_____

_____

_____

_____

_____

_____

_____

_____

_____

_____

_____

_____

_____

_____

_____

_____

_____

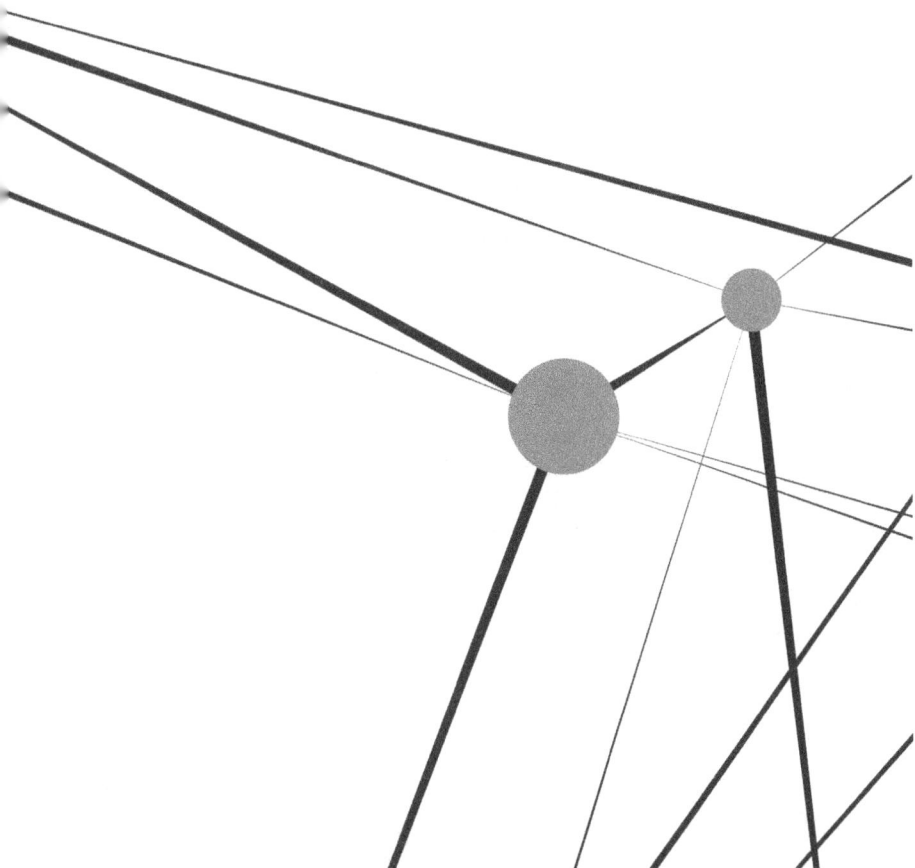

PETER

Passion

Ice-breaker Question:

Imagine you are a superhero. If you could have only one superpower what would it be? How would you use it to help others?

Video Clip: Follow along questions for video (fill in the blank)

1. If you are going to compare yourself to anybody it should be _____ _____.

2. Peter was an _____ fisherman who was quick with the _____.

3. The thing that characterized Peter most is _____.

4. Passion, like any tool, when used _____ can do a lot of _____.

5. Passion has to be coupled with the right _____. The _____ must be the head of it.

6. If you want to experience _____ in your life like Peter, you must love the Lord your God with all your heart, with all your _____, with all your _____, and with all your _____ – and with passion!

Group Questions and Exercises:

1. Read Luke 5:1-11. Put yourself in Peter's position. How would you feel being asked to put the boat back in the water after not just a long night's work, but a night where you had worked with nothing to show for it? What would your reaction have been when the nets started to break? When the boats began to sink?

2. Peter is often remembered for his impulsiveness. Read the following passages and describe Peter's errors. Split the verses up and have each person or small group share their answer. Matthew 14:25-31, 16:21-23, 17:1-6, 26:31-35, 26:69-74, John 18:1-11

3. When Jesus first runs into Simon He renames him "Peter," which means "rock." You just looked at many of Peter's faults. Jesus knew every one of them and, yet, He saw past them and knew that Peter would be a pillar for the disciples. What does Jesus' perspective of Peter teach us about how God sees us?

4. Very often, man's greatest strength is also his greatest weakness. Peter's hastiness got him into trouble sometimes, but he was also very decisive and lived life PASSIONATELY! When Jesus asked Peter to follow Him, Peter didn't give it a second thought. He left his nets and his boat on the shore and followed Jesus! When Peter saw Jesus on the water he leapt out of the boat! Romans 12:11 says "never be lacking in zeal, but keep your spiritual fervor, serving the lord." Go back to the "ice-breaker" questions from the beginning of this section and think about your answer to the question, "How would you use your power to help others?" Do you think that your answers reflect what you are passionate about? What real-world efforts could you make to serve in those areas?

5. How cool is it that Jesus takes Simon Peter back out in his boat to teach him. Isn't it awesome to know our God meets us where we are at! And He often uses what we already know to help us better understand His truth. What would it look like and what tools would He use if Jesus came to where you work in order to teach you? What questions would you ask Him?

Prayer Directive:

1. Father, forgive me for the times in my life when I have been impetuous or even reckless. So often I try to move in my own strength instead of listening for your voice and trying to discern the path you desire for me. Help me to slow down. Help me to be patient and wait on you.

2. Father God, help me to remember that I am to rejoice in you always. I pray that I will have a renewal of spirit today, that I will go out into the world with a passion for life, and exalt your name in all that I say and do!

JP Takeaway: Journey Principle and Action Steps:

	PURIFY	AMPLIFY	MULTIPLY
PETER **PASSION**	As we saw with Peter, sometimes your greatest strength can also be your greatest weakness. Ask God for purification and focus so that your passion reflects His.	Hone your craft. Cultivate your passion so that it can be used in the most effective ways in the most advantageous avenues. This is accomplished by continually seeking the Lord's will and growing closer to Him.	This one could also be titled "testify!" Passion has a ripple effect, so share your testimony and let your passions ignite the passion in others! Watch how the results are multiplied.

Notes

_____

_____

_____

_____

_____

_____

_____

_____

_____

_____

_____

_____

_____

_____

_____

_____

_____

_____

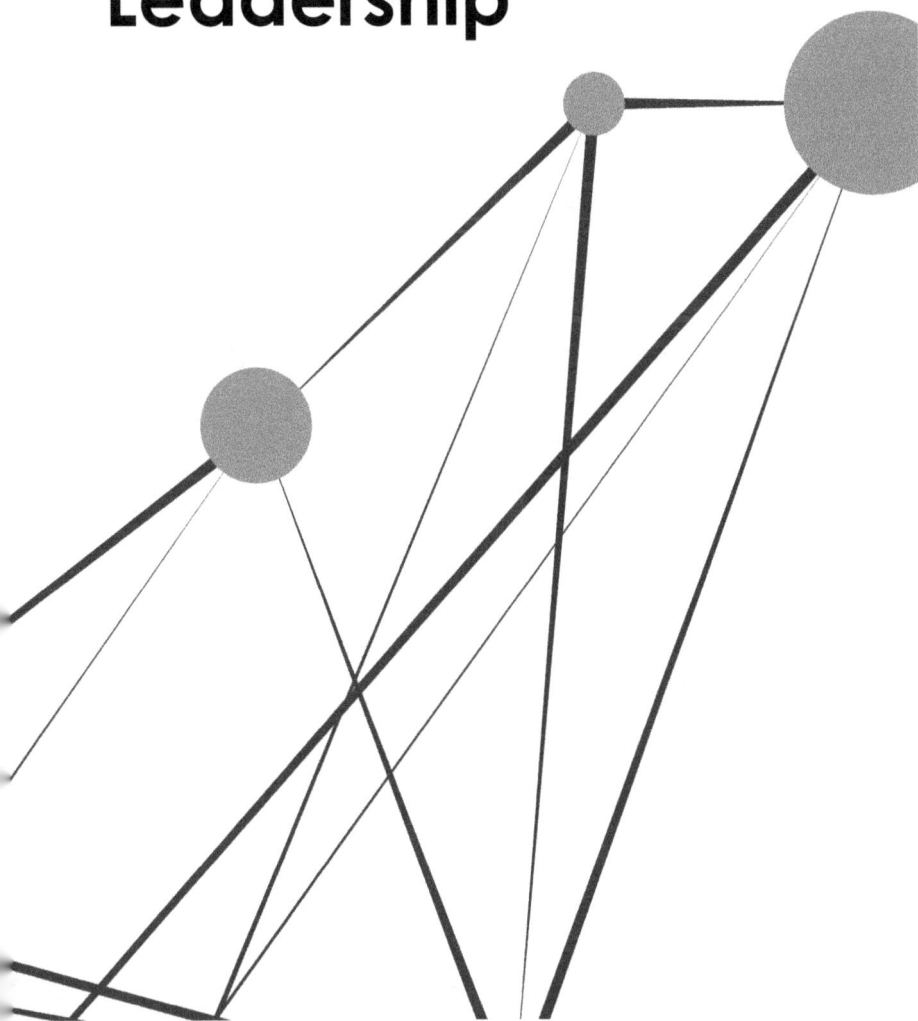

PAUL

Leadership

Ice-breaker Question:

Has there ever been a time in your life when a door was closed abruptly? Maybe you even thought you were on the right path, but God stopped you in your tracks? Did you understand what you were being told/shown in the moment or did it take some time to be able to look back and see it as a blessing?

Video Clip: Follow along questions for video (fill in the blank)

1. Saul was blinded by passion, _____, and _____.

2. Stephen says he was "keeping people from Jesus by _____ his fingers at them."

3. Talents that are not funneled through _____ are wasted and fruit not offered through _____ waste away in time.

4. Leadership starts with _____.

5. A true leader meets people where they are at instead of coming from a position of _____.

6. Study after study shows that leaders with the best results practice _____ _____.

Group Questions and Exercises:

1. Paul's upbringing – raised in a multi-cultural environment (Roman, Greek, and Hebrew), able to speak multiple languages, and given a top notch education (Torah and classical) where he was taught by perhaps the most noteworthy rabbi in the New Testament, Gamaliel – made him a prime candidate for sharing The Gospel in any location and with any cultural or religious background. Try to think about the specific ways in which you were raised. What about your upbringing, your education, or your life experience has equipped you to share the Gospel of Jesus Christ?

2. Building off of Question 1, has God given you a passion for a specific ministry? Think about your testimony. Think of how God has worked in your life. Does seeing what God has done for you

give you a desire to reach out to those who may have be in a similar situation, environment, etc.? Discuss ways that these gifts might be able to be put into practice.

3. Paul was zealously hunting believers before being blinded on the Damascus road. Think about the type of change in your life that would take you from a place of hate to compassion. How would you expect those you persecuted to react? What single trait do you believe would best equip you to handle the transition?

4. I love how Ananias comes to Paul. Paul had become such a well-known oppressor of Christianity that surely Ananias knew who Paul was. Yet, despite the possibility of Paul having him arrested, Ananias is obedient to God's commands and lays his hand on Paul, prays for him, and then baptizes him in the name of Jesus Christ. Is there a time in your life when God sent you a spiritual guide to help you through a time of "blindness" (Paul's perspective)? Is there a time in your life when it seemed like following God's command put you in danger (Ananias' perspective)?

5. Paul was an amazing leader! There are so many examples in his writings that express his character, but there is one section in Acts that ties up much of who Paul was as a man in a tight little bow. Read Acts 20:17-36 and try to list all of Paul's character traits that are shared in this short passage alone. Discuss how each trait translates into leadership?

Prayer Directive:

Pray: Father God, you have a plan. Long before I ever took a breath in this world you crafted me with your hands. My entire life, every cherished memory and every moment of pain is a brush stroke in your perfect design. Thank you that, like Paul, my past can't separate me from you Lord. Thank you that even though I have spent a lifetime running in every direction, but yours, my aimlessness and my recklessness can still be redirected into your flawless will. When the enemy whispers the guilt and shame of my past into my ear, I will not listen! I know that every wound, every trespass that he would try to use against me is a powerful weapon in the hands of my sovereign Lord. So use me, Father. Let my testimony humbly reflect your unfailing, unending, unstoppable, unconditional love!

JP Takeaway: Journey Principle and Action Steps:

	CONNECT	DIRECT	PROTECT
PAUL LEADERSHIP/ BOLDNESS	Leadership starts with relationship. A true leader meets people where they are at instead of coming from a position of authority. Study after study shows that leaders with the best results practice servant leadership.	Communicate a clear objective and the path to achieve it. Express direction with boldness, but enforce it with compassion.	Protection can mean having someone's back, but it also means protecting them from themselves. Practice accountability! Also, make sure you are providing the right tools for success to protect against failure.

Notes

_____

_____

_____

_____

_____

_____

_____

_____

_____

_____

_____

_____

_____

_____

_____

_____

_____

Thoughts and Reflections

_____

_____

_____

_____

_____

_____

_____

_____

_____

_____

_____

_____

_____

_____

_____

_____

_____

_____

Answer Key

Lesson 1 - Daniel
1. Uprooted, Babylonian
2. Dress, Eat
3. Serve, Wisdom, Strength
4. Misfit, Purpose
5. Shake
6. Persevere, Adapt

Lesson 2 - Jacob
1. Struggled
2. Stew
3. Fourteen
4. Determination, Stubbornness
5. Strengths, Weaknesses
6. Laziness, God

Lesson 3 - David
1. Valor, King, Prophet
2. Murderer
3. God's Own Heart
4. Repentance
5. Renounce, Renew

Thoughts and Reflections

_____

_____

_____

_____

_____

_____

_____

_____

_____

_____

_____

_____

_____

_____

_____

_____

_____

Answer Key

Lesson 4 - Abraham
1. Give You, Obedient
2. Grace
3. Uncomfortable, Grain
4. Love, Obey
5. Sacrifice

Lesson 5 - John
1. Jesus, Love
2. Washing
3. Fear
4. Moments, Relationships, Patient
5. Static

Lesson 6 - Ruth
1. Husband, Kids
2. Boaz
3. Determine
4. Accountability

Thoughts and Reflections

_____

_____

_____

_____

_____

_____

_____

_____

_____

_____

_____

_____

_____

_____

_____

_____

_____

Answer Key

Lesson 7 - Elijah
1. Frustration, Anxiety
2. Obedience
3. Gifts
4. Stuff, People

Lesson 8 - Jonathan
1. Loyalty, Sword, Belt
2. Covenant, Whatever
3. Kill, Gap
4. Honesty
5. Foundation, Durable

Lesson 9 - Rahab
1. Top, House
2. Kindness, Promise
3. Unlikely, Prostitute
4. Redemption, Confess
5. God, Her Entire Family

Thoughts and Reflections

_____

_____

_____

_____

_____

_____

_____

_____

_____

_____

_____

_____

_____

_____

_____

_____

_____

_____

_____

Answer Key

Lesson 10 - Aaron
1. Moses'
2. Staff
3. Kindness
4. Irritated
5. About
6. Value

Lesson 11 - Peter
1. Jesus Christ
2. Uneducated, Mouth
3. Passion
4. Incorrectly, Harm
5. Leadership, Lord
6. Transformation, Soul, Mind, Strength

Lesson 12 - Paul
1. Pride, Arrogance
2. Pointing
3. Faith, Grace
4. Relationships
5. Authority
6. Servant Leadership